Mr S

Written by Julia Donaldson
Illustrated by Celia Canning

I made a ball,
a ball of snow.

I made my snowball grow…

and grow.

I made a snowman
big and fat.

I gave him buttons
and a hat.

I made his eyes.

I made his nose.

I made his arms.

I made his toes.

When I went in
to have my tea,

he threw a snowball
after me.

I made a ball,
a ball of snow.
I made my snowball grow
and grow.
I made a snowman
big and fat.
I gave him buttons
and a hat.
I made his eyes.
I made his nose.
I made his arms.
I made his toes.
When I went in to have my tea,
he threw a snowball after me.